SKILLS FOR SUCCESS™

STRENGTHENING TEST PREPARATION SKILLS

ALEXIS BURLING

Rosen
YA™

New York

Published in 2018 by The Rosen Publishing Group, Inc.
29 East 21st Street, New York, NY 10010

First Edition

Library of Congress Cataloging-in-Publication Data

Names: Burling, Alexis, author.
Title: Strengthening test preparation skills / Alexis Burling.
Description: New York, NY : Rosen Publishing, 2018. | Series: Skills for success | Includes bibliographical references and index.
Identifiers: LCCN 2016053793 | ISBN 9781508175742 (library bound)
Subjects: LCSH: Test-taking skills—Juvenile literature. | Study skills—Juvenile literature.
Classification: LCC LB3060.57 .B86 2017 | DDC 371.26—dc23
LC record available at https://lccn.loc.gov/2016053793

Manufactured in the United States of America

CONTENTS

INTRODUCTION

Let's be honest. In most situations, taking tests isn't exactly fun. Sure, staying up late to finish a gripping novel for English class or listening to a fascinating lecture about Japanese history are both engaging activities. But taking a quiz on the material the next morning? That can be downright stressful.

The notes you took in class need interpreting and there are flashcards to make. Memorizing facts, figures, and important dates can sometimes take hours, if not days. Getting a good night sleep and balancing study time with homework is tricky, especially when you'd rather be hanging out with friends.

On top of all that, there's the anxiety that comes with actually taking the test. Finishing a multiple-choice exam on time and answering all the questions is essential. So is remembering to express your thoughts clearly and confidently in short-answer questions and essays. But learning how to master these skills isn't impossible. In fact, with just a few adjustments to your daily routine, you can become a test-taking whiz in no time. All it takes is just a little practice—and a heaping spoonful of patience.

In this resource, you'll be introduced to a variety of ideas about test-taking habits. Some—such as notic-

Taking tests is tough. But don't let anxiety ruin your concentration or lower your score. Put your best foot forward by paying attention in class and starting your study routine early at home.

ing and owning up to your weaknesses—might seem uncomfortable in the beginning. After all, maybe you're not aware that analogies and algebra problems aren't your strong suit. Coming to terms with your limitations is a difficult process. But it is an important first step to getting on track when it comes to preparing for exams. It also makes self-improvement possible.

Other theories presented in this resource might appear unrelated but could be a springboard to a whole new approach to academics. You might ask yourself: "Does it really matter that I'm listening to music while studying?" "Does an average of eight hours of sleep and a well-balanced diet actually impact test performance?" (Hint: In both cases, yes.)

Above all, the goal of this resource is to help you raise your test scores—and boost your confidence along the way. Not every suggestion will apply to your specific situation. But with step-by-step instructions and tips on everything from effective time management to learning how to bounce back after failure, the following chapters aim to provide you with the practical tools you need to become your best self at school.

Plus, solid SAT or ACT scores and good grades on your high school transcript can help you get into the technical school or college of your choice. For those of you who are interested in heading straight into the workforce, the easy-to-digest strategies discussed in this resource will also help you thrive on the job. Learning how to prepare for tests—or any situation in which you might be asked to demonstrate your knowledge on a subject or idea—is a key stop on the journey toward success.

Know
Thyself

Imagine you are prepping for an exam with multiple-choice questions and an essay. Aside from a few sick days, you have gone to class. You have read and taken notes on the material and lectures. You have done the homework. Now it's crunch time. Consider the following five statements:

- "There's too much information to review. I don't know where to start."

- "I've put in some time studying, but it doesn't matter. No matter how hard I try, I always do poorly."

- "I took notes but don't understand what I wrote down and am too afraid to ask for help."

- "I did the work but my memory is terrible. What subject is this test on again?"

- "I think I'll ace the multiple-choice section. But the writing portion? Forget it. It's hard to string thoughts together and my essays usually read like gobbledygook."

Do any of these sound familiar? If so, you're not alone. Many students are not at their best going into a test. Some aren't confident in their abilities. For others, the trouble starts earlier—by not developing productive listening habits in class. But just because you might identify with one or more of the above statements does *not* mean you're a lost cause. All it takes is figuring out what your optimal learning style is. Then you can use that knowledge to your advantage when getting ready for an exam.

WHAT'S MY LEARNING STYLE?

There are many philosophies about how people take in, understand, and retain information. After all, every person learns differently. But one of the most widely accepted theories was developed in 1987 by a university professor in New Zealand named Neil Fleming. In a research paper entitled "Not Another Inventory, Rather a Catalyst for Reflection," he described a new way of learning called VARK, which changed the way educators approached teaching.

According to Fleming, VARK consists of four key learning styles: visual, auditory, reading/writing, and kinesthetic. Let's define these one at a time:

- Visual learners use tools such as maps, graphs, charts, and images to help them comprehend and remember new information.

- Auditory learners take in information best when they're

Professor Neil Fleming's research suggests that visual and reading/writing learners process information best when it is clearly written down, something they can see with their own eyes.

listening to lectures and audio recordings or participating in group discussions.

- Reading/Writing learners most enjoy anything having to do with words, whether it's reading a textbook or taking notes.

- Kinesthetic learners are all action. They might try to understand how something works by taking it apart and putting it back together.

FRAMING YOUR MIND

When it comes to teaching, there are many opinions about whether the concept of "learning styles" holds any merit. Some education experts, like biology professor Tanya Noel, claim there isn't enough proof that the theory works. "There is ample evidence that teaching toward preferred learning styles does not seem to actually help people learn," Noel posted on her blog, The Nucleoid. "Many teachers/professors and students waste time and energy on this, efforts they could be directing elsewhere."

Other teachers believe there are more than four styles of learning. Some follow educator Howard Gardner's teachings. In his book *Frames of Mind: The Theory of Multiple Intelligences*, published in 1983, Gardner describes seven styles of learning. In addition to the four types used in VARK, he calls for three more:

- Interpersonal: Learners who thrive on interpreting feelings and moods, communicating with others, and socializing in order to process information.

- Intrapersonal: Learners who are independent thinkers and prefer to solve problems and work on projects alone rather than in groups.

- Logical-mathematical: Learners who think about concepts and approach projects logically and methodically, using reason.

After reading through Fleming's list think about the way you prefer to learn information. Ask yourself: Does any particular style stand out more than the others? If you can, pick out the one that most closely describes your personality and habits. Keep in mind that you might be a mix of two (or even three), depending on the situation. Got it? Good. Now that you understand how you process new facts and concepts, you can use that knowledge to manage your time in class and when studying.

For example, say you're an auditory learner. Perhaps bringing a recording device to class would improve your memory when it comes time to studying the material.

Auditory learners thrive on communication. They retain information more easily when they're given the chance to listen to others' opinions and share their own ideas.

Replaying lectures given by your teacher, then reciting the information aloud at home, is a great way to keep what you learned in your brain.

If you're a reading/writing or visual learner, you might choose a different route. Try taking detailed notes as your teacher is talking. Then, when it comes time to study for the exam, rewrite the information in a different notebook. You can also create a series of infographics and mnemonic devices to help you recall the information. These methods might sound time-consuming. But you'll be surprised how simple it can be to use your preferred learning style(s) to your advantage.

For all students, taking detailed notes during class is key. It helps you remember the facts and keeps your thoughts organized when studying.

KICK YOUR STRENGTHS UP A NOTCH

The next step in learning how to "know thyself," at least when it comes to demonstrating your smarts on a test, is remembering why you're great. Sure, you might be famous at school for having the most legendary outfits in your grade. Or maybe the sound of your singing voice as you saunter down the hallways causes the opposite sex to swoon. But how about when it comes to academics? Where do you excel?

Take a look at your last transcript. Are there any As? If so, bravo. Pat yourself on the back. These are the subjects in which you shine. Whether it's math, English, social studies, or band, getting an A means you've put in the necessary energy to prove you know your stuff. In most cases, it also means you're passionate and care about what you're learning.

In addition to pumping up your morale and making your parents proud, acing a class is also important for two other reasons. First, it means you've already developed positive paper-writing or test-taking habits that are working to your benefit. Keep up the good work and chances are you'll continue to do just as well, if not better, in future semesters. If you can, try using those same effective methods in other classes.

Perhaps more important, consistently earning As in certain areas could also be a signal that you may not need to spend as much energy studying for those particular tests or classes. Of course, don't stop making an effort altogether. But

This may sound obvious, but consistently earning good grades in a class means you're doing something right. Pinpoint what works and spread those skills around so you can improve in other areas.

redistributing your attention will enable you to focus more heavily on subjects where your performance isn't as strong.

Did you write an A+ paper that you're particularly proud of? Did you ace a geometry test that took weeks of preparation? Way to go. Take a magnet and post it on the refrigerator or tack it to your bulletin board. It might seem corny, but acknowledging your accomplishments can do wonders for your self-esteem. It's also a great way to motivate hard work in the future.

SAY YES, THEN NO TO WEAKNESSES

We all wish we could be Wonder Woman or Superman. Who doesn't want to succeed at everything we set out to do? But let's get real. No one is perfect. Just as we all have strengths, we have weaknesses, too—especially when it comes to school. And taking tests? For many of us, it can be a real challenge.

The easiest way to figure out areas where we need to improve is to make a list. Start by writing down all your strengths. Then make a second column to the right and jot down all the tasks you find to be difficult. For example, maybe you write excellent papers but you're terrible at multiple-choice. Or it could be that taking written exams in Spanish is a breeze, but giving an oral presentation? That's a different story.

Whatever the case may be, keep the VARK learning styles in mind when creating your list. And remember: Be truthful about where you stand. Whether you're an A+ student or a C- student, studying for a test or preparing for a job interview, there's no point in exaggerating your assets or ignoring flaws. It'll only waste valuable time and diminish your chances for success.

Now look over your list. See the column on the right? Those are the areas that need your undivided attention. While it might seem overwhelming now, don't give up yet. By working to your strengths—and owning up to your weaknesses—you're already well on your way to lifting your test scores and creating positive habits that will benefit you over the course of a lifetime.

CHAPTER TWO

Lights, Camera, Action

You have identified your learning style. You're being candid about areas where you excel and those that need improvement. Now it's time to get down to business and develop an action plan.

Think of it like auditioning for the lead role in a movie. First, you have to look the part. Maybe you style your hair in a certain way or wear the style of jeans the character might wear. Then you figure out how to walk, talk, and even think like your character. You do this by researching everything you can about the role—your character's favorite music, food, or book. Finally, you "become" the part by putting everything you learned into practice and making the character come alive. Then, when it's time to actually audition, you're strong, confident, and ready to go. Why? Because you've done the work and prepped for success.

It's the same with taking tests. For most of us, doing well on an exam doesn't just happen automatically. It takes dedication and careful planning. The process begins in the classroom.

BECOME A CLASS ACT

It's a no-brainer that your time in the classroom is important, especially when it comes to test prep. So why not become the best student you can be—not just on Tuesdays, but all year round. The first part is easy: start by showing up to every class. A perfect attendance record is the key to getting good grades. The only time when cutting class is excusable is if you're sick or dealing with a family emergency. If you do have to skip a day, make sure to find out from friends what you missed. Ask your teacher for the homework assignment and get copies of lecture notes on any critical material

The model student shows up to class and completes his or her work on time. Success in school means holding yourself accountable.

The next step is a two-part process: be an active listener and take smart notes on what you heard. Learning how to become an active listener is simple. It means staying alert and paying close attention to detail at all times. If your seats aren't assigned, try sitting as close to the front of the classroom as possible so you can see the board and hear what the teacher is saying. Though it might be tempting to sit next to that cute girl you've had a crush on for ages, doing so will only distract you from learning. Save your flirting for the lunchroom.

Whether you're taking notes on a laptop or in a notebook, tune in to what your teacher is saying and think about how it relates to what you've been studying during the rest of the year. Don't just write *everything* down. Try to evaluate which facts are significant and take clear, organized, and thorough notes on the topic being discussed. If there's anything you don't understand, don't be afraid to ask questions. Participate in class discussions by contributing your thoughts and listening to what others have to say. Keep your mind focused and daydreaming to a minimum. Most important, if electronics are allowed in class, turn off your cellphone. Getting a text from that cute boy might do wonders for your self-esteem, but it certainly won't be useful when it's time to take your science test.

Lastly, do your homework. Though it might eat into valuable time with family or friends, staying on top of assignments and turning them in on time is a key compo-

For the modern student, after-school activities take up a ton of time. But don't forget to schedule an hour or two for homework. Getting assignments in on time will boost your final grade.

nent to preparing for a test. Homework demonstrates your understanding of a subject. It shows your teacher how well you know the material. It also highlights areas where you need to improve. Completing a homework assignment is almost like a rehearsal for a performance. When it comes time to take the actual test, you'll have a deeper grasp of the information when it counts.

STUDYING CAN BE FUN. REALLY.

As a young person, you have a lot of responsibilities on your plate. Maybe you're the captain of the soccer team or play bass in a band. Perhaps you're on the yearbook committee or a member of the student council. Then there's everything outside of school—taking care of siblings, keeping up with a part-time job, and, of course, hanging out with friends. How do you stay on top of everything and still get good grades? By forming healthy routines.

The easiest way to succeed on a test is to form effective—and lasting—study habits. If that sounds boring, it doesn't have to be. In fact, figuring out how to make studying work best for you can almost be, yes, fun. Think back to your learning style. Are you a kinesthetic learner? Try reciting the names of World War II battles for the upcoming history quiz aloud while playing basketball with friends from class. If you're a reading/writing learner, make flashcards at least a week before the test and run through them every day on the bus to and from school.

How and where you study is important, too. Some students retain information best by working with a study buddy or in groups. Others need to work alone in a quiet space without any distractions—no music or television playing in the background, no munchies allowed. Whatever the case may be, it's a smart idea to figure out what kind of situation works for you and go with it. Whether in the library, outside, or at home, create a space—or multiple spaces—where undisturbed studying is possible. Fill it with your favorite blanket or pillows for optimum comfort. But whatever you do, don't fall asleep. If you feel your eyes closing or thoughts drifting, take a fifteen-minute break or switch to a location where you can stay focused. Studying for a test may not be your favorite activity, but it doesn't have to be tedious.

BEAT THE CLOCK

Everyone knows there are 24 hours in a day. But raise your hand if you use every one of those hours wisely. Is your hand still resting in your lap? If so, that's not surprising. Most, if not all, kids and adults have less than perfect time-management skills in most areas of their lives. Thankfully, there are ways to fix this problem.

The simplest path to managing your time more effectively is to create a daily or weekly to-do list either on paper or electronically on your phone, tablet, or computer. It might seem annoying at first. But jotting down everything you need to take care of when studying for an exam—homework, chores, social activities—will force you to keep track of goals and help you complete each activity in a timely fashion. There's also another benefit: crossing out each item when it's done. Drawing a physical line through a to-do task can give you a sense of accomplishment. It also prompts you to shift your focus to the next job or assignment.

Use a calendar to create a master schedule of all your assignments, upcoming tests, and project due dates. Then, add in the fun stuff: extracurricular activities and plans with friends.

In addition to your running list, coming up with a daily or weekly schedule can help you stay organized and reduce stress. Block out time for reading or writing papers. Then pencil in any after-school activities. Finally, mark down the dates of every test you know about. In the week leading up to each one, dedicate at least 45 minutes to an hour every night to studying. That time can be spent rereading material, making flashcards, going over concepts with a study group, or testing yourself on what you know.

Perhaps the most rewarding tip to keep in mind when developing time-management skills is remembering to leave room for "me time." Take a walk around the block. Have a snack. Listen to some music. Or call a friend for a chat. Studies show that taking breaks between study sessions strengthens your memory, lifts your spirits, and keeps your body relaxed.

CRAM SHAM

Studies show that procrastinating and waiting until the night before to study for an exam is a recipe for disaster. In addition to raising anxiety levels, it's also nearly impossible to fill your brain with everything you need to know in such a short period of time and have it stick.

As you probably can relate, most young people's lives are busy. Sometimes it's not possible to dedicate a week or more to test prep. If you do have to cram, here are some smart ways to go about it:

- Don't pull an all-nighter. Staying up all night will only make you tired. An exhausted brain makes remembering information difficult.

- Keep caffeine and sugary drinks to a minimum, especially late at night. Drinking sugary soda can cause you to crash when it counts most.

- Don't try to accomplish the impossible. If you haven't read all the material, don't try to do so the night before. Stick to skimming and taking notes on important details. You may not get every answer right. But answering a few questions confidently and correctly is better than trying to remember everything and retaining nothing.

A little "me time" can be a good thing. Jamming out to music, baking some cookies, even taking a stroll in the park can help break up the monotony of studying.

HEALTH MEANS WEALTH

According to the National Sleep Foundation, most young people have irregular sleep patterns during the week. They stay up into the wee hours of the night and get up at the crack of dawn the next morning to get ready for school. To make up for lost time, they sleep in late on the weekends, sometimes until 1:00 p.m. This seesaw effect can change their biological clocks and interfere with the quality of their sleep.

Does this ring a bell? If so, it's time to adjust your sleeping habits. The National Sleep Foundation recom-

MEDITATION NATION

Studying for tests, let alone actually taking them, can be a nerve-frying experience. When you feel stressed out, it also causes ailments in your body. Sore shoulders, back pain, and tummy trouble are not that uncommon.

When preparing for a test, take time out of your day to treat your body kindly. Do some careful stretching. Take twenty minutes to run through a yoga routine. Listen to calming music while lying flat on your back on the floor.

If you're open to it, meditating can do wonders for your memory. It helps you discard unimportant information and leaves your mind feeling relaxed. Make sure to close your eyes, breathe in through your nose and out through your mouth. Sit for at least ten minutes, if not longer. If you keep up the practice, you'll be amazed at how your academic performance and attitude improves over time.

mends eight to ten hours of sleep each night in order to function. One study by the foundation showed that only 15 percent of teens reported falling into this category. If you're getting less than eight hours sleep on most nights, it's time to adjust your schedule and make sleep a priority.

In addition to sleep, getting plenty of exercise is also necessary to performing well on a test and keeping your

Practicing meditation or yoga helps calm the mind and strengthen the body. Many students report doing better on tests after they've formed a weekly or daily routine.

brain sharp. According to the Physical Activity Guidelines for Americans issued by the US Department of Health and Human Services, children and adolescents ages six to seventeen should have at least an hour of physical activity each day and aerobic activity—like running or playing some sort of sport—at least three days a week. The guidelines also emphasize muscle-building and bone-strengthening exercises like push-ups, lifting weights, or squats. Many studies have shown that students who are physically active tend to have better cognitive performance, classroom behavior, and higher scores on tests.

A healthy, well-balanced diet is important, too, which means three solid meals a day. According to the Centers for Disease Control and Prevention, skipping breakfast is associated with decreased attention spans, alertness, problem-solving skills, and information-processing abilities. Diets low in vitamins A, B6, B12, C, folate, iron, zinc, and calcium can lead to low academic performance.

If you want to become a more effective learner, try ramping up your diet. Eat meals that include fruits, vegetables, whole grains, low-fat protein, and dairy. Avoid fatty foods like potato chips, processed junk food, or cookies. And most important, keep sugary snacks like candy or soda and meals high in sodium, like packaged soups, to a minimum. Healthy stomachs mean healthy brains.

CHAPTER THREE

Asking for Help

Whether you're in school or on the job, certain high-pressure situations can cause nervousness. Will the hours you spent behind the wheel help you pass your driver's test? Will weeks of drilling lines inspire a flawless performance as the lead in your school's annual musical? When it comes to prepping for an exam, sometimes it can seem bewildering to attempt the task all on your own.

That's why asking for help is crucial. Depending on your goals and comfort level, there are many ways to do so. From your peers to guidance counselors to online courses, making the most of the resources available to you can go a long way in squelching your anxiety and help you keep track of your progress.

USE YOUR TEACHERS

The most obvious go-to person for help on an exam is, of course, your teacher. After all, your teacher is the one who makes up the questions. But using your teachers as study

Your teachers are ideal test-prep resources. They can fill you in on which types of questions might be on the exam and explain concepts you might have missed.

aides isn't as simple as demanding: "What's on the test?" (They probably won't disclose that information anyway.) Instead, try to ask more general but targeted questions to help you figure out which material to focus on while studying. Here are a few examples:

- What is the format of the test? Will there be multiple-choice questions? Short-answer or essay questions? If so, how many?

- How many points will each question be worth? Is each section of the exam weighted equally?

- Will there be any extra-credit questions?

- How much will the test count in my overall grade?

- Is the exam cumulative or only on material covered since the last test?

- Do you have any suggestions on which material I should concentrate on most heavily or which methods might be most effective when studying?

In addition to specifics about the exam, you can also ask your teacher questions about any material you didn't understand from your reading, homework, or lectures. Sure, it can feel awkward to admit you aren't grasping certain concepts. But being honest about what you *don't* know shows your teacher that you are interested in learning and care about being a good student. It also demonstrates maturity.

Keep in mind that timing is important. Although approaching a teacher for help during class is always acceptable, the best time to do so is either after class or during office hours, if that's an option. This way, you won't be interrupted by other students. Your teacher will likely have more time to focus on you individually. Plus, because you're showing initiative, he or she might give you more detailed clues about the exam.

STUDY GROUPS: PROS AND CONS

Teachers are busy people. They have lessons to prepare and meetings to attend. Plenty of students count on them throughout the school day. So if your teacher is unavail-

Are you cramming for an exam and don't want to go it alone? Forming a study group of like-minded students can kick your grades up a notch by fostering collaborative learning.

able to help you prepare for a specific exam, don't fret. There's another option that might come to your rescue: the study group.

Study groups are a smart way to accomplish two tasks at the same time: studying and socializing. If you choose your group wisely, you'll not only benefit from each member's learning habits but also enjoy yourself in the process. For example, one of your classmates might be an excellent note taker and have information others missed. Another might have a firmer grasp of a certain subject and can explain it to the group. Even answering follow-up questions from your peers can help you flesh out the holes in your knowledge. By describing a concept to others, you gain a better understanding of the topic.

Being a member of a dedicated study group also means people are depending on you—for information and emotional support. Why is that important? Because it means you'll let others down if you don't hold up your end of the bargain. Treat the meet-ups like a job. Show up on time. Create clear goals beforehand and stay organized. Participate in review sessions and take a leadership position when appropriate. Stick to the agreed-upon schedule and get as much out of every gathering as you can. By bringing your best self to the table, you'll get positive results in return.

CHOOSE OR LOSE

Are you forming a study group? Do you need to spice up your group's test-prep sessions? Try following these simple methods for staying on track and maximizing your potential prior to test time:

- Keep study groups to between four and six people, ideally those who want to get good grades and not just friends. The smaller the group, the more you can take advantage of each other's strengths when preparing for tests. This way, everyone participates equally.

- Schedule meetings in areas where you won't be distracted. School libraries or a classmate's basement are both great choices. While a café might be more fun, it's also much easier to get sidetracked by music, other people, and the hustle and bustle of a restaurant.

- A two- to three-hour window is best for group study sessions. Shorter meet-ups can sometimes feel too rushed. Longer meetings can drag on. They key is staying focused for the duration.

- Meet at the same time every week, if possible. That way, everyone in the group can plan other activities accordingly and keep cancellations to a minimum.

- Choose a leader each week to run the meeting. This ensures that everyone is held accountable for the material, but it doesn't dump the responsibility all on one person. Hold elections the week prior to every session. Or have a sign-up sheet where people can volunteer to lead when it best suits their schedules.

If you have difficulty studying alone, joining a study session can give you the structure and motivation you need to do well. But there are some drawbacks to watch out for. For one, if you're the only student in your group who takes thorough notes, you'll waste more time filling everyone else in and run the risk of not receiving help in return. Make sure there's an equal give and take.

Secondly, if your group is made up of friends, take extra care to maintain focus. The temptation to goof off is strong. Try building some time into the schedule for an unstructured half-hour break or impromptu dance party. This way you can save all of your socializing for then and be more productive during work hours.

GOING PRO: CLASSES AND PRIVATE TUTORS

In certain situations, such as studying for an extra-hard calculus midterm or prepping for the SATs, drastic circumstances can sometimes call for drastic measures. Maybe you already met with your teacher and still need additional help. Or maybe your attempts to form a productive study group fell through. Whatever the case may be, seeking external help such as an online class or a private tutor can be a fruitful part of your action plan.

Let's start by tackling these options one at a time. If your family has the means to do so, hiring a private tutor is a great step for auditory learners and students who prefer one-on-one instruction. Why? Because lessons are tailored to your specific needs. Tutors can come in many forms. Some might be local parents. Others are librarians or professionals in your community. If there's a university nearby, its campus career center is worth visiting because college students often tutor middle and high school students for extra cash. The cost of hiring a tutor varies. You can do some research on the Internet to find out the range of hourly rates in your area.

College students make excellent private tutors. They often charge less than professional companies and can offer great tips on what to do first and test traps to avoid.

If a class setting is more your speed, there are hundreds, if not thousands, of options available, depending on where you live. National organizations such as Kaplan and the Princeton Review offer standardized test-prep classes throughout the United States and in some parts of Canada. These courses will teach you strategies on how to study and take the PSAT, SAT, ACT, and AP subject tests using actual

TEST-PREP RESOURCES THAT WON'T BREAK THE BANK

It would be great to win the lottery, right? But everyone knows that money doesn't grow on trees. Having a tiny or nonexistent test-prep budget doesn't mean you're doomed to failure. You just have to be smarter about the tools you use.

Luckily, teachers and professionals all over the world are working to create affordable online resources to help make learning easy, less stressful, and fun. Plus, with technology constantly evolving, more are popping up every day. Here are just a few:

- March2Success provides free self-paced study programs in math, English, and science, and focuses on material learned in grades 8–12. Sample SAT and ACT practice tests and information on college scholarships and financial aid are also available.

- Working alongside the College Board, Khan Academy offers free SAT test-prep strategies and interactive practice exams to all students. Online courses on everything from algebra to computer programming are also available.

- A low-cost alternative to expensive SAT and ACT classes is eKnowledge. Programs are available online or on DVD. They include more than eleven hours of video instruction and more than three thousand files of additional test-prep material.

- CollegeSpring partners with schools and community organizations to help students from low-income backgrounds boost SAT scores. Mentors also help students navigate college admissions and financial aid applications.

sample exams for practice. They also provide students with results-driven tips on applying to college and offer one-on-one help via email, phone, or live chat. Though the cost and duration of each class varies, most are expensive and require a rigorous commitment. For example, the Princeton Review offers a SAT-review course. It meets multiple times a week for six weeks.

Finally, for reading/writing learners or for those who don't have extra money to pay for test-prep classes, there are plenty of print and online resources available for little to no cost. Every standardized test you'll need to take during your middle and high school career has a test-prep guide or textbook. The Internet also contains a seemingly endless variety of education-oriented sites, such as PrepScholar, Coursera, and MathTV.

Whether you're studying for the TOEFL exam or just want to brush up on a topic for an upcoming geometry quiz, check out your library or local bookstore for help.

CHAPTER FOUR

It's Test Time

Most people don't like taking tests. This is a fact. But if you have gotten this far, it means you're interested in doing well and improving your test scores. You've put in the time to get organized for the big day. Let your confidence shine.

But before heading to class or the testing center, there are just a few more strategies to keep in mind. Most important, remember to set your alarm clock the night before your test. Place the clock across the room so you'll be forced to get out of bed. Use alarms from two different devices if you are worried you'll oversleep. Or ask a family member or friend to give you a wake-up call. If you're a chronic snooze button user, set your alarm early enough to allow for the extra time.

Give yourself enough space to get dressed without feeling rushed. Go over the material out loud in the shower while you wake up to warm up your brain. Wear comfortable shoes and clothing. Drink a cup of coffee, if that's your preference. Eat a well-balanced meal that includes plenty of protein to keep you energized throughout the day. If you're old enough to drive and your exam is first thing in the morning, leave yourself at least fifteen minutes of wiggle room so you don't have to speed and can find a parking space. The last thing you want to happen is to get locked out of the testing room because you're late.

GET IN. GET READY.

Maybe your stomach is growling. Or maybe you're a little nervous you won't finish every question. But once you're in the test-taking room, it's time to set your anxiety aside. The final

Don't forget breakfast! A hard-boiled egg or a heaping bowl of yogurt with some fruit will keep your energy sky high throughout the morning.

preparation you should make is to ensure you have everything you do—and don't—need before the exam begins.

If you're taking a standardized test like the SAT or ACT and can choose where you sit, pick your seat wisely, just like you did in your classroom at school. If you are someone who is easily distracted, avoid sitting next to a window. Something happening outside might steal your attention away from the test. Be sure that you are either wearing a watch or can see a clock without having to get up from your seat.

Now that you're seated and comfortable, look inside your backpack to make sure you have taken out all the tools you might use throughout the course of the exam. If it's an on-paper test, take out at least two black or blue pens, or sharpened pencils depending on what's allowed. This way you'll have an extra one should the writing utensil you're using break or run out of ink. If you're taking a math test and regular or graphic calculators are permitted, put those on your desk, too. Extra batteries are useful to prevent any mishaps

Finally, keep a full bottle of cold water on your desk if at all possible. Unfortunately, most test-taking situations don't allow snacks or gum. Noisy wrappers can disrupt people's focus. But staying hydrated is an easy way to keep your thirst quenched and brain active over the course of a few hours. Just make sure to pace yourself so you don't have to get up and use the bathroom.

GENERAL TEST-TAKING STRATEGIES

Whether you're taking an objective test filled with fill-in-the-blank and true-false questions, an essay test, or a combination of both, there are a few general strategies to remember that will work in any situation. First, read through the entire exam to get a sense of the types of questions being asked and how the test is structured. Don't just dive in. This simple practice will enable you to map out a mental plan and help you decide how much time to spend on each question before moving on to the next section. It also minimizes any panic that could set in halfway through.

Next, as you are taking the test, be sure to read any set of directions very carefully. This means reading them all the way through—every time. Often directions contain important information you might need to be aware of before you begin answering questions. For example, many students lose valuable points by writing a response to just one essay when they're supposed to complete all three.

No matter how you're doing on the exam, remember to keep track of time. Steady pacing is key. If you find you're lagging behind, don't panic. Just try to pick up the pace. Never spend too much time on any one question. If you can, circle the number of any difficult questions you're having trouble with. Then go back and revisit these stumpers after you've tackled all the easy ones.

QUICK AND DIRTY TIPS

Even if you are a top-notch student, chances are you're not going to get every answer correct on an exam. But following a few simple tips will help you narrow down multiple-choice

In test-taking situations, remember to be mindful of the time as you go along. Spending too much time on any one section can prevent you from finishing with confidence.

answers, write clearheaded essays, and solve math problems with pizazz. Let's examine some of the most common test section types:

ACING MULTIPLE CHOICE

• Use the process of elimination. Start by looking for the wrong answer first. By weeding out the incorrect choices, you're already one step closer to the truth.

• Be careful with "all of the above" answer options. In order for this choice to be true, remember that every other answer must be correct. The same rule holds true for "none of the above."

• Pay attention to context clues. Words such as "but," "although," "therefore," and "because" can often help you cross out incorrect answers.

TACKLING TRUE-FALSE

- Take note of absolute words such as "never," "always," "everyone," and "none." These usually signal that an answer is false. Why? Because most statements aren't black or white. There is usually an exception.

- Alternatively, words like "usually," "sometimes," "many," or "frequently" often mean that the answer is true.

- Watch out for sentences that contain two true statements that aren't connected. For example: Babe Ruth is a famous baseball player because he played for the New York Yankees. Both parts of the sentences are correct, but Babe Ruth isn't famous *because* he played for the Yankees.

READYING FOR READING COMPREHENSION

- Browse through all the questions before actually reading the passage. Doing so will help you focus on the relevant information more quickly.

- If you can, highlight or underline key words or phrases while you're reading the passage. Then go back and find evidence to support the answer options.

- Pay attention to any charts, illustrations, or graphs that might provide additional information.

TO GUESS OR NOT TO GUESS?

As of March 2016, the SAT no longer penalizes students for incorrect answers. So if you're knee-deep into a standardized test and are stumped by a question, your best bet is to guess. But that doesn't mean you have to guess randomly. Try to be smart about your choices. Narrow down options. Don't overthink it. Always trust your instinct. If you're at a total loss, ask yourself which of the answers sounds most familiar. That one's most likely to be true. Another no-no? Going back and changing your answer. Unless you're completely sure your new pick is better, stick to your original decision. Studies show your first answer choice is more often the correct one.

MAKING MATH EASIER

- If you're figuring out a math problem that includes multiple-choice answer options, keep those in your head when doing your calculations. They might be clues to a short cut along the way.

- Show all your work. Use diagrams and illustrations to help you solve difficult word problems.

- Write legibly. Even if your answer is wrong, you may be able to receive partial credit in some testing situations.

If you're taking a Scantron test, be sure each bubble you fill in corresponds to the question you're answering. It's easy to miss a row, so stay alert.

WRITING WINNING ESSAYS

- Create a quick outline or jot down a few notes of ideas you want to include in your essay. This will help you stay organized so you can present your ideas in a clear and concise manner.

- Structure your essay like a paper you'd write for class. It should contain an introduction, a body consisting of a few short paragraphs, and a conclusion.

- Remember to make sure your thesis or topic sentence is strong and can support the ideas in the rest of your paper. Back up your ideas with plenty of evidence and facts.

REVIEW, REVISE, RELAX

As your exam comes to a close, it's tempting to either freak out and panic or waste the last few precious moments. But don't lose your focus. The final ten minutes can be extraordinarily helpful in bumping up your score, even if it's by just a few points.

Start by going back through the test and tackling any questions you might have missed. In most cases, it's better to fill in the answer rather than leave it blank. You have a one-in-four, or sometimes one-in-two, chance of picking the correct choice. Then, change any answers you might have filled in incorrectly. Remember: this often results in a wrong answer, so be especially careful in multiple-choice or true-false sections.

When you feel confident with your performance, turn the test in. Pack up your bag and leave quietly. Or, if you're in a classroom situation, sit tight until the rest of your peers are done. Then, and perhaps most important, take a deep breath, relax, and celebrate. You're done. It's time to treat yourself to an ice cream sundae or fun plans with a friend. Why? Because hard work should always be matched by a fabulous reward.

Be Your Own Boss

Congratulations! You're test-taking saga is over. But just because you're done filling in rows of tiny bubbles on a Scantron sheet or writing essays in French for your foreign language AP exam doesn't mean your job is finished. There's much more to be done. In fact, the steps you take *after* an exam will not only help you learn from your mistakes, they will also inspire you to form long-lasting healthy habits and set goals for the future. It's called being your own boss.

BOUNCE BACK

Getting good grades on tests and keeping up with studying is all about making positive choices. Being your own boss means managing your time effectively and having discipline. It also means holding yourself accountable to successes—and failures. If you aced your exam or wrote the perfect essay, keep up the good work. Your study habits paid off.

You handed in your exam. Doesn't it feel spectacular? Whether you aced it or feel you could've done better, there's always a "next time" to up your game.

If you didn't do as well as you had hoped, try not to get depressed or give up. Negative reinforcement can often lead to future failure. Plus, contrary to popular belief, one bad grade isn't going to ruin your chances for success—as long as it doesn't become a pattern. Instead, try turning the unfavorable situation into a positive one. If your teacher has time and is open to it, go over the answers you missed on the exam together. If it was a paper or essay, ask how you can improve. Remember, if there is anything you still don't understand by the end of the session, speak up. You'll never learn from your mistakes if you don't ask questions.

The most crucial part of becoming your own boss is knowing when it's time to adjust your actions to make them work to your advantage. For example, let's say you bombed your biology exam because you picked your boyfriend as your study partner and spent more time procrastinating than studying. Next time, don't wait until the last minute. Take note of all the decisions you made that *didn't* work for you and change them to behaviors that will benefit you in the future.

STUDY BUDDY OR BFF?

One common mistake many students make is choosing a best friend as a study partner. This isn't always a problem. But more often than not, it's hard to concentrate when there are so many other cool things to talk about, like music, your latest crushes, sports, and school gossip. Try picking a person with whom you can focus on work—someone who you can learn from and who will inspire you to do well.

On the flip side, it is also important to choose your friends wisely. Pals who push you to skip school and blow off homework are bad influences. No matter what the situation, true friends should be people who pick you up when you're feeling down and cheer to the rooftops when you succeed.

Cramming during lunch before the test could help you answer a few questions correctly. But it's not going to deliver a top grade. Don't procrastinate. Start studying early.

WELCOME TO THE "REAL WORLD"

Honing and strengthening your test prep skills is one of the most worthwhile goals you can set for yourself in middle and high school. Doing well on your transcript and mastering the SATs or ACTs to the best of your abilities will help you get into a good community college, trade school, or university. But the studying habits you form can also carry you beyond your education years and into the real world. They're the stepping-stones to building a solid career.

Model employees come in all shapes and sizes. But they do have a few characteristics in common, just like students. Whether they're the head of a giant corporation or an entry-level assistant, most successful professionals are excellent listeners and solid communicators. They budget their time wisely in order to keep

Business leaders are busy people. But they're not complacent. Becoming successful takes drive, courage, and a constant willingness to improve.

track of priorities. Many often juggle different projects over the course of a single day and sticking to deadlines is a must. Being able to work independently and collaborate as part of a team are two of the most important qualities employers look for when they're searching for potential candidates to hire.

Perhaps the most valued skill you can have as you start out in your career is something you also learned while prepping for a test: confidence and willpower. By owning what you know, admitting what you don't know, and working hard to accomplish your goals, you are destined to succeed. Good luck on your journey!

GLOSSARY

CANDID Expressing a thought or feeling in an honest way.

COGNITIVE A type of mental ability such as thinking, learning, remembering, and understanding.

CRAM To prep in a hurry for an exam.

DIMINISH To become smaller or less than, or cause someone or something else to do so.

FRUITFUL Abundant; producing a lot of something.

INFOGRAPHICS Images that use words, charts, and graphics to describe a concept or idea.

INITIATIVE The push or energy it takes to accomplish something or put a plan into action.

INTERPERSONAL Happening between people.

INTRAPERSONAL Happening within a person.

KINESTHETIC Having to do with moving one's body.

MEDITATION The practice of spending time in a quiet position in order to reflect or think; quieting one's mind.

MNEMONIC DEVICE A trick that helps a person retain information or improve memory.

OPTIMAL Ideal; best.

PROCRASTINATION The act of putting off doing something for another time.

PRODUCTIVE Working hard and in an efficient manner.

REDISTRIBUTE To spread or divide something up into different areas.

RELEVANT Appropriate; having to do with a thought or idea.

SQUELCH To do away with.

TEDIOUS Difficult or boring.

TRANSCRIPT A written record of a student's grades; a report card.

UNDISPUTED Universally accepted.

WILLPOWER The determination or energy to do or accomplish something.

FOR MORE INFORMATION

College Board
250 Vesey Street
New York, NY 10281
(212) 713-8000
Website: https://www.collegeboard.org
Made up for more than 6,000 educational institutions in
the United States, the College Board trains students
to take the SAT and ACT, and offers programs to help
students research, apply to, and finance the college of
their choice.

"I Have a Dream" Foundation
322 Eighth Avenue, 2nd Floor
New York, NY 10001
(212) 293-5480
Website: http://www.ihaveadreamfoundation.org

The "I Have a Dream" Foundation helps students in
under-served communities achieve their college and
career goals by teaching them crucial life skills and
provides them with the tools they need to excel in
school and beyond. Tuition assistance for higher
education is also guaranteed.

Kaplan, Inc.
6301 Kaplan University Avenue
Fort Lauderdale, FL 33309
(954) 515-3993

Website: http://kaplan.com
With regional branches all over the United States, Canada, and more than thirty countries abroad, Kaplan is one of the premiere test-prep and career-readiness companies in the world.

Library of Congress
Thomas Jefferson Building
10 First Street SE
Washington, DC 20540
(202) 707-8000
Website: https://www.loc.gov
The Library of Congress provides valuable research opportunities and resources for students, including millions of books, audio recordings, and historical records. It's also the largest library in the world, with three buildings full of comfortable places to study.

Oxford Learning
747 Hyde Park Road, Suite 230
London, ON N6H 3S3
Canada
(519) 473-1460
Website: https://www.oxfordlearning.com
With more than one hundred centers across Canada, Oxford Learning provides a variety of educational programs for students in preschool through high school, including instruction on how to conquer

homework assignments, study efficiently, and succeed in college or technical school.

University of California Early Academic Outreach Program (EAOP)
UC Berkeley Office
2150 Kittredge Street, Suite 3A
Berkeley, CA 94720-1060
(510) 642-2364
Website: http://www.eaop.org
Serving students at more than 150 K–12 public schools throughout California, EAOP boosts students' morale by teaching important job-related skills, helping them improve their academic standing, and guiding them through the college application, financial aid, and admissions processes.

WEBSITES

Because of the changing nature of Internet links, Rosen Publishing has developed an online list of websites related to the subject of this book. This site is updated regularly. Please use this link to access the list:

http://www.rosenlinks.com/SFS/testprep

FOR FURTHER READING

College Board. *The Official SAT Study Guide, 2016 Edition.* New York, NY: CollegeBoard, 2016.

Covey, Sean. *The 7 Habits of Highly Effective Teens.* New York, NY: Touchstone, 2014.

Crossman, Ann. *Study Smart, Study Less: Earn Better Grades and Higher Test Scores, Learn Study Habits That Get Fast Results, and Discover Your Study Persona.* Berkeley, CA: Ten Speed Press, 2011.

Fry, Ron. *Surefire Tips to Improve Your Study Skills (Surefire Study Success).* New York, NY: Rosen Publishing, 2016.

Fry, Ron. *Surefire Tips to Improve Your Test-Taking Skills (Surefire Study Success).* New York, NY: Rosen Publishing, 2016.

Hollsman, Jessica. *The High School Survival Guide: Your Roadmap to Studying, Socializing & Succeeding.* Coral Gables, FL: Mango Publishing, 2016.

Maats, Hunter, and Katie O'Brien. *The Straight-A Conspiracy: Your Secret Guide to Ending the Stress of School and Totally Ruling the World.* Los Angeles, CA: 368 Press, 2013.

Muchnick, Cynthia Clumeck. *The Everything Guide to Study Skills.* Avon, MA: Adams Media, 2011.

Muchnick, Cynthia Clumeck. *Straight-A Study Skills: More Than 200 Essential Strategies to Ace Your Exams, Boost Your Grades, and Achieve Lasting Academic Success.* Avon, MA: Adams Media, 2013.

Rozakis, Laurie. *Super Study Skills: The Ultimate Guide to Tests and Studying.* New York, NY: Scholastic Reference, 2002.

Rozakis, Laurie. *Test-Taking Strategies & Study Skills for the Utterly Confused.* New York, NY: McGraw-Hill. 2003.

Weisman, Stefanie. *The Secrets of Top Students: Tips, Tools, and Techniques for Acing High School and College.* Naperville, IL: Sourcebooks, 2013.

BIBLIOGRAPHY

Centers for Disease Control and Prevention, "Health and Academic Achievement," May 2014. https://www.cdc.gov.

Centers for Disease Control and Prevention. "Youth Physical Activity Guidelines Toolkit," August 27, 2015. https://www.cdc.gov/healthyschools/physicalactivity/guidelines.htm.

EducationCorner.com. "Study Skills for Students." Retrieved September 28, 2016. http://www.educationcorner.com/study-skills.html.

EducationCorner.com. "Using Study Groups." Retrieved September 28, 2016. http://www.educationcorner.com/studing-groups.html.

Ellis, Julie. "8 Inspiring eLearning Websites That Offer Students Inspiring Educational Alternatives." eLearning Industry. https://elearningindustry.com.

Mangrum-Strichart Learning Resources. "Study Skills Articles." Retrieved September 28, 2016. http://www.how-to-study.com/study-skills-articles.asp.

Markarian, Margie. "Checklist: Test-Taking Strategies for Middle and High School Students." Scholastic Inc. Retrieved September 28, 2016. http://www.scholastic.com.

Nast, Phil. "Test Prep & Review Strategies for Grades 9–12." National Education Association, March 7, 2016. http://www.nea.org/tools/lessons/Test-Prep-Review-Strategies-Grades-9-12.html.

National Sleep Foundation. "Teens and Sleep." Retrieved September 28, 2016. https://sleepfoundation.org/sleep-topics/teens-and-sleep.

North, Anna. "Are 'Learning Styles' a Symptom of Education's Ills?" *New York Times*, February 25, 2015. http://www.nytimes.com.

Nutrition.gov. "For Teens and Tweens," September 22, 2016. https://www.nutrition.gov/life-stages/adolescents/tweens-and-teens.

Open Culture. "200 Free Kids Educational Resources: Video Lessons, Apps, Books, Websites & More." Retrieved September 28, 2016. http://www.openculture.com/free_k-12_educational_resource.

The Princeton Review. "The New SAT. We're ON IT." Retrieved September 28, 2016. http://www.princetonreview.com/college/sat-changes.

Rhone, Nedra. "Free and Affordable Test Prep Options for the SAT and ACT." AJC.com, September 22, 2016. http://www.ajc.com.

Savage, Lorraine. "Top Five Questions to Ask Your Professor Before Your Final Exam." Cengage Brainiac, April 1, 2014. http://blog.cengagebrain.com.

Staffaroni, Laura. "The Best Way to Review Your Mistakes for the SAT/ACT." PrepScholar, April 30, 2015. http://blog.prepscholar.com/the-best-way-to-review-your-mistakes-for-the-sat-act.

Staffaroni, Laura. "How Much Should You Pay for SAT/ACT Tutoring?" PrepScholar, April 16, 2015. http://blog.prepscholar.com/how-much-should-you-pay-for-sat-act-tutoring.

Sylvan Learning. "Study Skills." Retrieved September 28, 2016.http://www.sylvanlearning.com/blog/index.php/tag/study-skills.

Teach.com. "Learning Styles: All Students Are Created Equally and Differently." Retrieved September 28, 2016. https://teach.com/what/teachers-teach/learning-styles.

VARK Learn Limited. "The VARK Modalities." Retrieved September 28, 2016. http://vark-learn.com/introduction-to-vark/the-vark-modalities.

INDEX

ABOUT THE AUTHOR

Alexis Burling spent many years as an editor and contributor to Scholastic's preeminent classroom magazines, including *Storyworks*, *Choices*, *Math*, and *SuperScience*. She now makes her living as a full-time writer and book critic and has published dozens of books for young readers on a variety of topics ranging from current events and biographies of famous people to test-prep and career advice.

PHOTO CREDITS